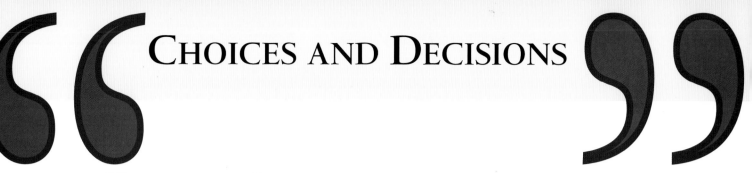

CHOICES AND DECISIONS

Dealing with Bullying

Pete Sanders

Aladdin / Watts
London • Sydney

© Aladdin Books Ltd 2004

Designed and produced by
Aladdin Books Ltd
28 Percy Street
London W1T 2BZ

New edition
first published in
Great Britain in 2004 by
Franklin Watts
96 Leonard Street
London EC2A 4XD

ISBN 0 7496 5494 5

Original edition published as
What Do You Know About –
Bullying

A catalogue record for this
book is available from the
British Library.

Editor
Katie Harker

Designer
Flick, Book Design & Graphics
Simon Morse

Illustrator
Mike Lacey

Picture Research
Brian Hunter Smart

CONTENTS

How to use this book

The books in this series deal with issues that may affect the lives of many young people.

- Each book can be read by a young person alone, or together with an adult.

- Issues raised in the storyline are further discussed in accompanying text.

- A list of practical ideas is given in the 'What can we do?' section at the end of the book.

- Organisations and helplines are listed for additional information and support.

INTRODUCTION

" In hindsight I know that the bullying wasn't my fault. But at the time, I blamed myself. I also tried to hide the fact that I was being bullied from my parents. "

It can be difficult to understand the real effect that bullying has on people. Some people who are bullied may become quiet and moody, or appear nervous and depressed. They might even pretend to be ill, to try to avoid the bully.

This book will help you to find out more about the causes and effects of bullying. Each chapter introduces a different aspect of the subject, illustrated by a continuing storyline. The characters in the story are involved in situations which affect many people in their everyday lives. After each episode, we stop and consider the issues raised, and open out the discussion. By the end of the book, you will know more about different ways of dealing with bullying and be able to make your own choices and decisions about how to act when faced with bullying.

That's it. They've gone too far.

WHAT IS BULLYING?

> A lot of bullying goes on at my school.
> But it's not always the hurting kind.
> A day doesn't go by without some kid
> being teased or called names.

You may already have a good idea about what bullying means. You may have been bullied yourself. You may even have bullied others. Bullying seems to happen everywhere, and to lots of different people.

There are also many different kinds of bullying. Bullies might use words, or they might hurt others physically. Sometimes they demand money or property. You probably know bullies who have tried to take friends away from people and make them feel lonely.

Bullies will often pick on somebody who will not fight back, or who they think will not tell anyone about them. Sometimes bullies say they are 'just teasing' or 'just playing' to try to excuse what they are doing. Remember that any kind of action which causes hurt or upset in others is serious, and should not be allowed to continue.

Some people don't always take bullying as seriously as they should. Sometimes this is because they don't know exactly what is happening.

Luke Simpson had a reason for arriving at school early...

... Glancing around the playground, he spotted Andrew and called him over.

This is the last time I can do this.

We'll see about that.

Once he had the money, Luke made his way to the school building. Nobody was allowed in before nine o'clock, so he knew the building would be empty. He needed a quiet place where he could count the money from Andrew.

I hope it's enough.

Whoever's in here had better come out now.

As Luke counted the money, he heard footsteps outside.

Luke knew he would need a good excuse for having so much money.

Luke had spent the morning worrying about what excuse he could give the principal, Miss Bass. But she had an unexpected visitor.

I'll tell her my mum gave it to me to buy a present for my grandma's birthday.

Mum, what are you doing here?

Luke knew he couldn't tell the truth.

Luke refused to say anything. Miss Bass decided to keep the money with her until he told the truth. She told Luke she would see him later.

Your mum and I are still waiting to hear where you got the money from, and what you want it for.

Luke dreaded telling Josh Stone why he didn't have the money. After all, today was the deadline.

Whoever's in here had better come out now.

Bullies often choose places where adults won't see them.
Possible danger areas might be the school bathrooms, the playground, the streets outside school or the school stairs. You might be able to think of other places where bullying happens.

Bullies usually pick on somebody who will not fight back. A bully might:

- push you around.

- call you names.

- hurt you by fighting with you.

- make fun of you and your family.

- talk about you behind your back.

- try to get money from you.

- threaten you in different ways.

- damage or steal your property.

- try to make you do something you don't want to.

- influence others not to be your friend.

- make sexist or racist comments about you or your friends.

WHY DO PEOPLE BECOME BULLIES?

> "I was quite unconfident at school. I used bullying as a way of making myself feel part of a gang. I picked on shy kids because it made me feel like I was the confident one."

Bullies like to be powerful. Sometimes they may be jealous of others, and use bullying as a way of getting at them. Bullies will pick on anyone if they think they can get away with it. They will look for situations which allow them to do this.

People become bullies for all kinds of reasons. Some people have very fixed ideas about what bullies are like. However, bullies are not just bigger boys making trouble. Some may be copying something that is happening to them at home – after all, adults can be bullies too. Or it might be their way of trying to look important in front of others.

Often people who are being bullied will bully others. This can lead to a kind of 'chain' of bullying. You may know of people who bully younger brothers or sisters because they feel helpless in other situations, where they think they do not have any power.

It's not always easy to spot a bully. Some bullies just don't look the type.

Josh was furious...

... Luke had been avoiding him all day. Now he was determined to find out why Luke had spent so much time in the office.

We don't need wimps like you in our gang. You're dead if you ever tell.

Luke tried to explain what had happened, but Josh was even more angry when he found out why Luke did not have the money.

The next day...

... Josh told the gang that Luke had been caught. Soon they were making up stories about him.

Let's call him Luke the puke.

That's a good one, Josh.

Luke still hadn't told his mum about Josh. He had become very moody. But he wasn't able to fool his mum for long. Now he dreaded going back to school.

A week later...

Why won't you tell me what is bothering you, Luke?

If only I could tell someone the truth.

... Luke's mum was convinced that he was pretending to be ill to avoid having to go to school.

What do you think the truth is?
Do you think Luke should tell someone?
How do you feel about Josh?

If only I could tell someone the truth.

Being bullied can make you feel very alone.
Some people lie about being bullied. You might even blame yourself, and believe you deserve to be bullied. You may also be forced to do things you don't want to do, such as stealing, and this often makes you feel much worse. Nobody should have to put up with feeling lonely and guilty in this way.

You're dead if you ever tell.

Bullies use fear as a weapon.
Some bullies use force to frighten people into doing what they want. Others use less obvious methods. They may threaten not to be your friend, or to let you be part of their gang. All bullies have one thing in common – they rely on people not telling on them.

STANDING UP TO BULLIES

" As soon as I stood my ground, the girls picked on me less and less. I suppose I had taken the fun out of their bullying. "

You may have heard grown-ups say that it is important to stand up to bullying. Challenging a bully can seem very difficult, but once you give in to a bully's demands it can be hard to stop.

If you are being bullied there are several things that you can do. Some people will tell you to deal with bullies by appearing confident, or by ignoring the situation and staying out of danger areas. It is up to you to to judge each situation and decide how best to deal with the problem.

Sometimes it's right to stand up for yourself, and refuse to do what the bully is demanding. At other times, it may be best to leave a situation. Once bullies

think they cannot exert power over you, they will probably back down and not pester you again. If you see someone else being bullied you should try to confront the bullies and question their behaviour.

Judge situations carefully, and don't allow yourself to be forced to do anything you are not happy with.

Mrs Simpson had noticed that some money had disappeared from her bag. She decided to leave some money on the table, to see what would happen.

I hope I'm wrong about this.

I think we need to have a long talk, Luke.

Luke was caught red-handed.

I can't tell you who they are, Mum. They'd beat me up if I did.

Luke was sorry for stealing the money. He felt guilty, and blamed himself for what was happening.

Please don't tell anybody. It'll be a lot worse for me at school.

Luke told his mum that he was being bullied, and that he had been given one last chance to be in the gang.

If Mum comes to school they'll know I've told on them.

Luke was glad he had told his mum, but he spent that night worrying about what would happen next.

What do you think Luke's mum will do?

Talking to people can help. It is important to know that from time to time you will meet situations which you cannot handle alone.

> I think we need to have a long talk, Luke.

Not talking to someone can often make the situation feel much worse. You may be afraid to say anything because it looks like you are 'telling tales'. If you are being bullied, talking to somebody about it is not telling tales. No one deserves to be bullied.

Bullies need help too.

Bullying can become second nature, and old habits are hard to break. If bullies are not helped with their behaviour, they may continue to bully all their lives.

> I can't tell you who they are, Mum.

Telling the right person
Some adults or friends will be better able to help than others. If you are being bullied, it is worth thinking carefully about who to tell. This might be a favourite teacher, or a parent.

WHAT WILL HAPPEN IF I TELL?

> " I didn't want to tell anyone. It was my problem and I had to fix it on my own. But then my teacher found me crying at school. It was a relief to tell someone about what was going on. "

When something goes wrong, most people try to work things out for themselves. Bullies rely on this. They know that it is often difficult to tell others, and this is particularly true as you get older.

Once you are aware that you can no longer handle the situation yourself, you may decide to tell someone. You will want to be sure that the bully cannot get back at you for having told the truth. Trusted adults will help to make sure this does not happen. Lots of schools have developed ways of dealing with bullying. They know it is important that the rules are fair to everyone. Some schools get parents and children involved in making the rules. Most schools know that bullying will not just go away by itself. They want everyone to be able to feel happy and safe.

Bullying can happen everywhere. Most schools will try to help people to deal with bullying for themselves.

The following day...

Thank you. I'll be there at ten-thirty.

Miss Bass talked to Mrs Simpson for a long time about what the school did about bullies.

I promise we won't single Luke out.

... Luke was pleased that his mum had agreed to see Miss Bass when everyone would be in class. He was still feeling very nervous.

Miss Bass said she would find out who was responsible.

It's a lovely day out there. The fresh air will do you good.

I couldn't get anything for you. Mum's even stopped my allowance.

Because he had no money for Josh, Luke tried to stay in at break time. When he couldn't, he tried to stay close to the teacher on duty.

Luke expected to be beaten up. Instead, Josh called him names and made fun of his family.

I told you so. He's not worth wasting time on.

How do you think Luke feels?

15

... Luke was making new friends from another class.

Luke watched as Josh and his gang played their usual tricks. He felt really sorry for Andrew.

Luke decided to tell Miss Bass. She would listen to him and be fair.

What do you think Miss Bass will do?

Most grown-ups will try to help you to stand up for yourself.

A few people think that bullying and being bullied are a part of growing up. But you have the right to say 'no' to someone who is bothering you. Most adults will encourage you to have the confidence to stand up to a bully.

I'm really pleased you came, Luke. I know it couldn't have been easy.

Adults cannot always tell that you are being bullied, even if it feels obvious to you.

It is not 'telling tales' to discuss your problem with someone. Bottling things up can make things worse.

I can't believe I was so concerned about being in Josh's gang.

Sometimes the idea of belonging to a gang is actually more exciting than the reality.

You may think you are missing out on something by not being in the gang. This is not always true.

HOW DO SCHOOLS DEAL WITH BULLYING?

" There are many reasons behind bullying. At our school, we have found that some children bully because they are upset or angry. "

Most adults agree that bullying is wrong, and they realise how difficult it can be to tell the truth about being bullied. They also know how important it is to try to protect the person who is being bullied.

Bullies must be helped to understand the effect of their behaviour on other people, and how it makes those people feel. Adults will try to find out why a person is bullying. They will want bullies to think of better ways to handle their feelings. They will try to help the bully understand that, although they like him or her as a person, they cannot allow the bullying to continue.

Everyone has the right to enjoy life without being threatened or made to feel small. Everyone needs to feel cared for and protected.

Everyone else can go for now.
Josh, I'd like you to stay.

After questioning everyone for a long time, Miss Bass knew that Josh was the leader.

I hope you understand how people feel because of what you've been doing.

Miss Bass talked to Josh for over half an hour.

No one's got any time for me at home anymore.

Josh told Miss Bass his mum was always busy with his new baby sister, and his dad was hardly ever there.

Miss Bass now understood a little more about Josh's bullying. She knew that habits like this were hard to break.

Let's talk again, Josh. We need to work hard to stop this bullying. I'll speak to your parents about the situation at home.

Back in the playground...

It's your fault. I'll get the blame for this.

... Luke did not try to avoid Josh. Although he was nervous, he felt strong enough to stand up to him.

Luke understood Josh more now, and actually felt sorry for him.

Go ahead and try. You're not so big without your gang to back you up.

The next day...

... was the last day of school before the summer holiday.

I'm really sorry.

Luke felt badly about having bullied Andrew.

Josh did not chase after him. Luke felt pleased with himself for standing up to Josh.

He wanted to make it up to Andrew if he could.

If any of them pick on you again, just let me know.

If any of them pick on you again, just let me know.

Is it okay to be in a gang? Being part of a group can be a lot of fun.

It's great to share good times together, and lots of people enjoy the feeling of confidence that joining in with others can give them.

Gangs can encourage bullying.

There are times when gang members go along with ideas, not because they want to, but because they are afraid of being bullied if they refuse. By simply allowing bullying to happen, the other members of the gang become bullies too.

Go ahead and try. You're not so big without your gang to back you up.

Standing up for yourself.
You might believe something is wrong with you if you are being bullied. This is not true. You do not have to go along with other people's ideas if you don't think they are right for you. In the end you have to respect yourself.

WHY DO SOME PEOPLE GET PICKED ON MORE THAN OTHERS?

> " Being the new girl was really difficult. It took a while to be accepted as part of the group. "

You may have thought about how difficult it is for new people to fit in. They may not know anyone. It can be hard to make new friends, particularly if the rest of the class know each other well.

Newcomers are sometimes missing old friends and familiar situations. They could well be feeling nervous and unsure. They might even behave in unexpected ways because of this. You may have known newcomers who even bully others, or join in with bullying to become accepted by a particular group. Some schools know about this, and have tried to come up with ideas to support anyone who feels isolated and alone. Many schools are very strict about anyone who is made to feel bad because they come from a different culture.

Some schools have a 'buddy system', whereby newcomers are looked after by someone who knows all about the school.

That summer...

... Luke went to his grandmother's house at the beach. He enjoyed playing with one of her neighbours, Amanda. Amanda always listened to Luke.

> I was really scared, but I'm glad I stood up to them.

Luke told Amanda all about Josh and the gang. He was surprised to find out that Amanda had seen bullying at her school too.

Amanda's story...

> This is Latika, who's starting school today.

... A new girl, called Latika, had started at Amanda's school. Lots of the other girls made fun of Latika.

Amanda knew that the girls were being racist. They hadn't even bothered to find out anything about Latika. It just didn't seem fair.

A couple of weeks later...

> You wouldn't catch any of us eating that garbage.

> None of you have given her a chance.

Amanda felt annoyed with the others.

Amanda and Latika gradually became friends.

Now that Amanda and Latika were friends, the other girls made fun of them both.

That Saturday...

... Amanda and Latika went shopping.

Amanda was shocked. She was really annoyed about what the others had done. She spent all weekend thinking about what to do.

What do you think Amanda is going to do? What would you do?

24

You wouldn't catch any of us eating that garbage.

Girls will often tease or call people names when they are bullying.
Girls sometimes bully using physical violence in the same way as boys. But more often, girls will use words to hurt other people – by teasing or calling people names. They might try to take another girl's friends away and talk about her behind her back. Although it is more common for boys to bully other boys, girls can be bullies, too.

Boys usually fight more when they are bullying.
Boys think fighting makes them look big in front of their friends. Some boys think this is what is expected of them. Boys will often choose to fight rather than bully someone verbally with names. Many boys do not like to show their real feelings. They may have been told that boys don't cry. But showing your feelings is a sign of strength, not a sign of weakness.

RACIST BULLYING

> I was being bullied because I looked different. And that made me more determined to show my true personality – to show that I was just the same as everyone else.

Bullies will often pick on people simply because they are different in some way. It may be the kinds of clothes they wear, or the food they eat, or the neighbourhood they come from.

Bullies will use all kinds of tactics to hurt people's feelings. People can be singled out just because they wear glasses. Picking on somebody who is a different colour is a very common way of bullying. Some people believe they

People come from many different backgrounds. If we only look at the differences, instead of getting to know the real person, we are missing out on a potential friendship.

are better than others, just because they are from a different race or culture. Racist bullies will refuse to get to know the person they are bullying, and will concentrate only on the differences they believe exist between them.

Amanda told her favourite teacher about how the girls were behaving. She knew that this teacher would understand and try to do something about it.

Later that same week...

We've tried to ignore it, but it's getting out of hand now.

How do you think bullying makes you feel?

The class did some lessons on why people bully, and different ways of handling bullying.

Sometimes ignoring things can work, but not always.

The teacher organised a mediation session. The girls talked together about what had been happening.

I joined in because the others were doing it.

I feel really upset when they make fun of how I dress.

Everyone was given a chance to say how they felt. The girls began to realise they hadn't given Latika a chance.

It took some time...

... The girls knew they had been racist, and had snubbed Amanda, too.

And so we have decided to ask for volunteers to look after new girls and girls who are being bullied. We don't want anyone to be unhappy in our school.

Bullying goes on everywhere. I think our school did really well. We learned how to deal with it for ourselves.

Things began to get a lot better.

I wish we had the same kind of thing at my school. I know a lot about bullying and how it feels.

That September...

... It was the beginning of the next school year. Miss Bass was talking to the students about new beginnings. Luke had already made up his mind that he would like to help sort out the bullying at his school. He had collected lots of information about where to get help.

Schools have developed various ways of dealing with bullying.

School mediation programmes give people who are being bullied a chance to talk directly to the bully about their feelings. Bullies also have the chance to talk. Usually, a teacher or another adult is on hand to make sure that the meeting is fair, and to help people to talk about ways of solving the problem.

We don't want anyone to be unhappy in our school.

Some schools have a 'School Council'.

Representatives of each class meet with a teacher to discuss any problems or concerns. It is an opportunity for the students to have their say in what they would like to see happening in the school. It is also a way for teachers to find out more about the concerns of students.

WHAT CAN WE DO?

" The worst thing was knowing that my brother was being bullied and not knowing how best to help him. "

Having read this book, you will understand more about the causes of bullying and the effects that bullying can have on people's lives.

By now you will probably have your own thoughts about how you can help to prevent bullying. You know that you can stop some bullying by ignoring it, or by being confident enough to say 'no'. In other situations, it is best to tell an adult.

You know how bullying can make you feel, and that there are actions you can take to help to stop bullying. Any kind of bullying that is upsetting you needs to be dealt with. Sometimes this might be something you do alone; sometimes you will need the help of others. Judging a situation needs careful thought. Above all, you know that you can do something about bullying, even if it is not always easy to believe it at the time.

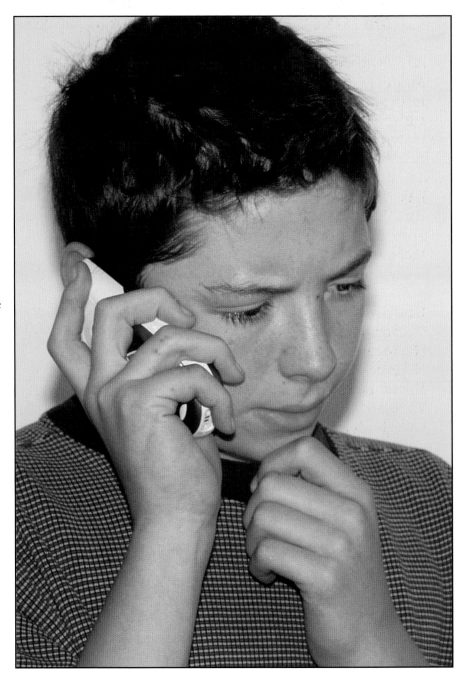

Bullying affects everyone – not just the people who are bullying and their victims. Those who know about bullying, or who watch it happen, are affected, too.

Adults and children who have read this book together may find it helpful to share their thoughts and ideas about the issues raised.

Sometimes adults need help with problems, too. Many of the organisations listed below provide information, advice and support for both adults and children. Nobody should have to put up with bullying. Together we can help to stop it.

Anti-Bullying Campaign
185 Tower Bridge Road
London
SE1 7UF
Tel: 020 7378 1446
Fax: 020 7378 8374

Anti-Bullying Network
Moray House School of
Education
University of Edinburgh
Holyrood Road
Edinburgh EH8 8AQ
Tel: 0131 651 6100
Fax: 0131 651 6100
Email:
abn@education.ed.ac.uk
Website:
www.antibullying.net

Bullying Online
9 Knox Way
Harrogate
N.Yorks HG1 3JL
Email: help@bullying.co.uk
Website:
www.bullying.co.uk

Careline
Cardinal Heenan Centre
326 High Road
Ilford
Essex IG1 1QP
Helpline: 020 8514 1177
Tel: 020 8514 5444
Fax: 020 8478 7943
Email:
careline@totalise.co.uk

Childline
45 Folgate Street
London E1 6GL
Tel: 020 7650 3200
Helpline: 0800 11 11
Textphone: 0800 400 222
Website:
www.childline.org.uk

Kidscape
2 Grosvenor Gardens
London SW1W 0DH
Tel: 020 7730 3300
Helpline: 08451 205 204
Website:
www.kidscape.org.uk

National Children's Bureau
8 Wakley Street
London EC1V 7QE
Tel: 020 7843 6000
Email:
membership@ncb.org.uk

National Society for the Prevention of Cruelty to Children (NSPCC)
Weston House
42 Curtain Road
London EC2A 3NH
Tel: 020 7825 2500
24-hour helpline:
0808 800 5000
Email: help@nspcc.org.uk
Website:
www.nspcc.org.uk

The Samaritans
The Upper Mill
Kingston Road
Ewell
Surrey KT17 2AF
Tel: 020 8394 8300
24-hour helpline:
0845 7 90 90 90
Email:
admin@samaritans.org
Website:
www.samaritans.org.uk

Beyond Bullying Association
PO Box 196
Nathan
Queensland 4111
Australia
Email: beyondbullyingassn@
ourbrisbane.com
Website: http://cwpp.slq.qld.
gov.au/BBA

Kids Help Line
PO Box 376
Red Hill
Queensland 4059
Australia
Tel: +61 (0) 7 3369 1588
Fax: +61 (0) 7 3367 1266
Email:
admin@kidshelp.com.au
Website:
www.kidshelp.com.au

No Bully
Website: www.police.govt.nz
/service/yes/nobully

INDEX

Photocredits
Abbreviations: l-left, r-right, b-bottom, t-top, c-centre, m-middle
All photos supplied by Roger Vlitos except for: Front cover – Select Pictures. 1, 10tl, 14b, 29t – Photodisc. 3b – Corbis.
7tl, 13t, 18b, 30r – PBD. 7br, 10b, 11br, 17br, 22r – Image State. 8b – Corbis. 13br, 21tr, 25br – Image 100.